BRAINSTORM

to Eddie

Brainstorm

Poems
By
M. T. Venti

Stella Luca Press
Key West, FL • Jackson, NH

BRAINSTORM

ISBN 978-0-9831811-1-8

First Edition

Stella Luca Press
PO Box 805, Jackson, NH 03846
http://www.StellaLucaPress.com

CONTENTS

One

Two

Three

One

SOLITUDINARIAN

Just before sunrise,
the moon in mid-arc over
mountain ridges. Air

thin and sharp. Black ice
coats the deck a dull sheen
that cracks under footsteps.

Snows tinge the tallest bald peaks
a pale yellow. Leafless trees,
trails glisten, white rivulets.

Frost crystallizes narrow roads,
pinches village houses.
Streetlights falter.

The bird feeder hangs
stiff, a fox's frozen track zigzags
into the woods. Nothing moves,

except steam from my coffee cup.

Why I Dream of the Galapagos Islands

In fifth grade, I was tall
in the back of the classroom, the windows
                cut sunlight into squares on the floor.

Covering one blackboard, geography maps
as big as the sheets
                on my mother's clothesline.

Sister Gabriel brandished a yardstick at Spain.
Outside on Pontoosuc Avenue, city workers dug and filled a hole,
                women pushed baby carriages,

cars stopped at the crosswalk. History is a series
of sailing ships plying flat oceans
                toward an unreachable horizon.

The Aztecs thought Cortez was Quetzalcoatl.
My mother was having another baby. I ironed and watched my sisters.
                Explorers splashed up on rocky coasts

guided by smoke curling from volcanoes.
Charles Darwin guessed the little finches' secret.
                God had no plan.

Extra points for good penmanship,
for daydreaming,
                ten whacks on my outstretched palm.

In the emergency room nurses shouted,
doors swung violently,
                me, with my sisters.

The chaplain baptized our baby brother
in everlasting happiness. How small,
                the white coffin my father chose.

"You have your own little saint," Sister Gabriel
 would tell me later.
                              In the bible story

God won his wager with Satan
 and rewarded Job with replacement children. Years,
                         like the little islands, stepping-stones.

MILL TOWN ELEGY

Icy mists drift in the river gorge,
her man down from the North Country.

Cigarette smoke mingles with
the sawmill's flume, sulfurous bite of dawn,

reminds her of hell… or forgiveness.
Shots and beers at Fagan's Pub, her man

concocts the reasons. Another
mission thwarted, the back of his hand

put sense into her. He knows a cop from school.
In *The Daily Sun*, a sentence or two

about broken glass, a neighbor's innuendo.
The moon-faced nun at St. Anne's shelter

serves sour coffee. Cluttering the pews,
plastic toys, magazines with pictures

of recipes and quiet streets. In this mill town
roads dead-end, sentinel pines cast their doubts.

By now her man is snoring on the sofa,
her apartment holds its breath. Someday

she'll steal a canoe, paddle to the ocean.
Dark currents wear away the bedrock,

mercury seeping through fissures, mill horn
and church bell drown each other out.

MAPPING THE STARS

       The soldier stares, his baby's ruddy fist
curling around the soldier's finger,
translucent fingernails longer than he imagined.
         None of it was planned.

       All night drive from Fort Bragg, a surprise.
Instead his girlfriend surprised him
with their son.
         She already knows this baby,

       his kicks, his refusal to turn, his husky cry,
his miniature skullcap
like a recruit. Her other gift, a planisphere
         to map the stars. They rise

       then pale in dawn's haze. On Route 95
the soldier captures memories of home—
piney woodlands, mottled cows, strip malls,
         her face as she soothes the baby—

       in his rear view mirror it all slips away. Nights
outside his barracks, the soldier turns
the planisphere's celestial wheel. Familiar stars rise
         along the edges of the Afghan mountains.

       Nights, sleeplessness cramps the house.
In the yard swing she sways the baby, whispers the myths
that dwell in the moonless sky. Stars shoot overhead
         like missiles burning toward morning.

FINITUDE

Green and indistinct all summer, suddenly
birches, maples and oaks
flaunt themselves in flares
of russet, orange, and especially gold.
Fireworks on the mountainsides.
No matter blinding cobalt sky
or soaking mist. Precious
is this new order.

Each trip to the market is a passage
through the rainbow's yellow band.
The only darkness, clusters of black pines,
granite outcrop, rain cloud.

Surrounded by vibrancy, urgency, impermanence.
I fear the shortening days
even before leaves flutter to the ground.
I stare, desperate to fix this memory
that stark branches and gray skies can't dull.
My heart musters acceptance.

Summit

That time we hiked up Mt. Washington,
fog clung to us like a wet sheet.

Trail cairns along the ridgeline vanished.
We nearly lost each other. You reached out

for my hand, map and guidebook, useless
in this rough country. Ravines cut by glaciers,

snow poised for avalanche. One
unthinking step could bring it down.

Water droplets needled us.
We crept hand in hand, mystified

within the forest's mossy scent.
Close by, a brook roared,

or was it the highway? Clouds
drifted in, then up. A sign

pointed the route down, *Lion's Head*.
Trail's end, or mirage? We shimmied

and slid down icy rocks.
Two split logs formed a bridge.

VESPERS

for Eddie

Evening's purple smudges the sky.
At this hour in medieval times, peasants
offered up their hearts to God.
In our halting isolation we murmur
into cell phones, adjust the radio.
A sharp exhale off the highway,
a roughly patched road
through salt hay marshes. Tidal
inflows beneath the causeway.
Shadowy birds fly off
like check marks from to-do's undone.
Tires crunch toward the garage light,
the sign you're already home,
my simple blessing at day's end.

Two

The Key West Cemetery

I

Pale lavender thickened with gray,
cumulus clouds curling upward above the edge
of the world. Not air, not water, not fire,
but all of these. On the island
we realize we were fools
to believe in anything but their presence.

II

Crypts and mausoleums like shotgun cottages
crowd eternity's neighborhood.
Cradled in their berths, the dead know
and do not blame. Abandoned at the portals
photographs forget how to grow old.
An angel stoops under marble wings,
her pitted face reads their histories:
senator, Cuban soldier, daughter,
longtime companion. "Beloved,"
their stones whisper. Under the harsh sun,
plastic flowers, spotted as overripe fruit.

III

We mourn the faded flamboyán.
Slabs crack and sink, forsaken.
On the path between graves
toppled sideways, a chipped vase.
Stars scatter across the sapphire sky
purposeful as souls.

Happy Hour

Rain happens, bouncing off pavement.
Frangipani blossoms flurry
like sweet-smelling snow.
I'm sheltered in a window seat,
my drink has a tiny umbrella.

A man pushes his rusty bike,
basket stuffed, something plaid,
a frying pan.
Gray water pooling in the culvert
washes over his bare feet.

On the third try he hoists the bike
onto the sidewalk. Through a veil
of stringy hair he glares
with the brittle dignity of age
or illness.

A crackle of thunder. The bar TV
flinches blank. Uneasy laughter.
A green caterpillar, shiny as a jellybean,
inches its way across the bands of dust
that stripe the screen.

La Bendita

I transcend sleep. My eyes,
the negative of my soul. Thoughts
collide like atoms, chaotic, critical.
From the far border of dreams
your deep sigh, the retriever sideways,
our bed a tangle of sheets, bodies, breath.
Night thins blue to gold, malleable
as a bracelet, reflective
as the diamond with its subtle flaws.
O mirror in the bathroom,
fill me with grace.
I am lion-headed, gap-toothed,
blessed among women.

WELCOME TO THE NEW WORLD

A metal heap launched from a Cuban beach,
wave-washed, erratic, in the Florida Straits.
Its salvaged Mercedes engine coughing
under a thirsty sun. Ocean breathing,
swells surround the balseros.

Madre de Dios! Visions, far, floating,
in the sky, specks, no shore in sight. Soon,
it must be tomorrow. Tonight,
the boat is iridescent as game fish.
No one dreams.

Drifting currents argue West then North
pushing the plough and stars. Horizon
long as a seawall.
A trick of dawn? Their paddles stir the sea,
thick as salty ajiaco.
Out of the blue,

specks wave back, beachgoers on A1A
jolted as the Calusa centuries ago,
bystanders to a vision offshore.

Arms reach out, hands pull them up,
wading, stumbling, wet feet to dry feet,
they barely touch the beautiful ground.
Each footfall, a rediscovery.

CASA MARINA

Fans wobble the lobby.
We swirl starry-eyed,
pale as tablecloths. Lush
fortress on a hidden beach,
the magnate's gift
to his railroad guests.

We swim, caesura,
shiny wavelet fingers tickle,
hammock-swaddled
lovers lost
in terry cloth robes.

The Casa's music echoes
outside its aura. Sunset
abandons the public beach
to gloom, slouched forms

intone their particular Angelus.
His beach is combed,
the magnate furrows in oil.

Breakfast arrives,
a waiter's lilting English,

our triviality.

WHEN THE WORLD WAS FLAT
OR WHAT I WISH MY MOTHER TOLD ME

Spin
until you fall into the damp earth's
grasp, an awakening,
you are part of it.

Open your eyes.
Trees tapering to blue,
clouds racing
over your flat world.

In the sun's simple brilliance,
Earth spins toward the future
revealing in evening the planets' sham.
Stars, all long dead or dying,
you won't believe.

Look up into blackness.
A dusty comet hurtles
through the interstellar sky,
a single-minded echo
from there to now.

The flash over mountains,
the foam on waves,
the glow behind clouds
like first light,
you.

See the leaves, scarlet and bloodless.

FACING THE SUN

I hate how this beach smells,
a fishy seaweed stew.
Coconut tourists
pawing at clamshell phones.
Palm trees like cheap fan dancers
flapping up everything.
Styrofoam rides an eddy
out to the sandbar,
take-out for mangy seabirds.
Such sights people pay to see.
Beyond ocean's steely distance,
blue rim under bluer sky,
a thin frontier of light.
Bathers far off shore,
burning silhouettes in tidal pools
almost walk on water.
Maybe I can change a little.

Three

BRAINSTORM

On bright days I am bewitched.
Sea too green, blank sun,
       reflection of a reflection,
       a place light turns inside itself.

       Islands abandoned to their verdure.
       Sailboats on gray horizons,
kindred clusters of little moth wings
flutter and bow toward the east.

A scorching vision.
I feel the solar wind on my skin.
       Ocean gulps and spits.
       Whirlpooling about, crashing,

       buoys like popped corks,
       channel markers toll.
At last, free to plummet.
Waves obscure applause,

sailors deflate, wings dissolve.
Armada to the party. Up
       down, luck, fluke, floating,
       pulled, the weight of expectation,

       brooding, like Icarus,
       his sunless sea deep as years.

SPLIT SCREEN

The woman overflows her wheelchair,
hospital gown draping to reveal
her grey bulbous breast. A tube forks
into her nostrils. Her companion, a heavy man,
wears his responsibility like family. He stares

at the TV on wall: *Little House on the Prairie*,
Laura at the church picnic.
A nurse chirps my name, "Strip to the waist."
The hygienic gown feels like the cape
from a cheap princess costume.

Two mechanized plates smooth as ice, grip.
The nurse, prattling about digital technology,
tightens, tightens. An image materializes,
my breast, a perfect apparition.

The woman's companion waits alone now, picking
at the wrapping on a butterscotch the same color
as his nicotine-stained fingers. Laura's sister and
a young man with a bolo string tie, his sudden push
toward the trees. Her screams are on mute.

TRAVELS

Getting cured makes you
too weak to go outside
so I bought a submarine
a small one, on sale.

Now we can travel protected against
infections, allergens, dirty rest stops.
We'll cook spaghetti with meat sauce and
breathe purified air while drinking red wine.

Through the periscope we'll see
Red Sox games, cousins' weddings, Sicily.
Sometimes you'll rest and I'll read aloud.
We'll take turns driving.

Afterward, you'll tell me to surface.
We'll motor on the sea,
bask in the sun's pale shadow
until it's time for one last dive.

St. Paul's

A small church with the heart of a cathedral
embraces its corner on Duval Street. Music
is the ministry on Sunday afternoons.

Flyers paper the gate with temptation,
classic rock at Hog's Breath,
two-for-one beers at The Bull & Whistle.

Thick doors open like arms welcoming
those who don't know what we are,
perhaps non-believers? Saints

from our childhoods stand silent.
The concertmaster orchestrates
introductions. Latecomers

slide to the center of pews worn glossy.
Cellos trill a familiar sonata,
the organ tremulant, mournful.

The choir pauses, in one breath
voices rise through the arches
like incense. Latin chants

unknowable as Christ on the Cross.
My soul vibrates with the bass,
not with faith, but something.

Phantasos Gallery Opening

A girder from a building that fell
is titled *Humanity*. The proprietress
recommends a papyrus watercolor: blue pasture
flowing up against purple strife, stopping.
His face is too red.
Black rockets sprout in a yellow cityscape.
From a tray I select a beggar's purse.

A gray-haired couple drinks white wine,
unmindful, glasses poised,
permanently. I feel
a prick in my arm. The bamboo tree's
dull leaf point, tiny pink flower.
In a wide room, imagined moonlight
curves over a chaise.

An invitation to still life.

ANNIVERSARY

Late-blooming roses
heed weather not time. Small joys
for waning days. They
bow from the glass vase somehow
unbroken year after year.

BEACH METAPHYSICS

My sun-whitened universe spins slowly,
orbiting in the snack bar's
gravitational pull. I'm burnt. Hot dogs ..
on their little Ferris wheel, sweat.
A chunky teenager with tongs
watches over them like a biologist.
Three bites and a napkin full of chips
daubed with mustard. Clouds, like words,
escape to the horizon. Waves
drag seaweed through my brain.
It's impossible to swim or diet.
Fringy pines lean westward,
signaling land to sailors lost off-shore.
On the picnic table my notebook pages
flutter witlessly in the wind. Today,
I wrote one good line.

ACKNOWLEDGEMENTS

Grateful acknowledgement to the editors of *The Secret of Salt: An Indigenous Journal*, in which the poem "Travels" appeared in a slightly different form.

Special thanks to my teachers and mentors at the Lesley University MFA Creative Writing Program: Steven Cramer, Teresa Cader, Thomas Sayers Ellis, Janet Sylvester, Spencer Reece, and in remembrance of Wayne Brown.

Thanks to The Studios of Key West (http://www.tskw.org). I'm proud to be a part of their artistic community.

And to Eddie, my first reader, with gratitude and love.